TO SEE HOW THIS BOOK & OTHERS IN THIS RANGE WERE STYLED TO MAKE STUNNING VISUAL STATEMENTS, & IMPROVE THE STYLE OF YOUR HOME THEN PLEASE VISIT:

- @ADJUSTANDACHIEVE - INSTAGRAM
- RENOVATION NATION - FACEBOOK PAGE

PLEASE TAG OUR INSTAGRAM ACCOUNT OR JOIN OUR FACEBOOK PAGE, & SHOW US HOW YOU HAVE STYLED A SPACE WITH OUR BOOKS, WE WILL BE GIVING OUT FREE PRIZES FOR THE BEST PICTURES.

GOOD LUCK!

Made in the USA
Las Vegas, NV
09 September 2024